MW01098393

GOURMET POPCORN

GEORGANNE BELL

ROM THE AUTHOR OF THE COOKIE COMPANION

GOURMET POPCORN
100 RECIPES FOR ANY OCCASION

GEORGANNE BELL

Front Table Books
An imprint of Cedar Fort, Inc.
Springville, Utah

ISBN 13: 978-1-4621-2154-0

Published by Front Table Books, an imprint of Cedar Fort, Inc.
2373 W. 700 S., Springville, UT, 84663
Distributed by Cedar Fort, Inc., www.cedarfort.com

LIBRARY OF CONGRESS CATALOGING-IN-PUBLICATION DATA

Names: Bell, Georganne, 1981- author.
Title: Gourmet popcorn : 100 recipes for any occasion / Georganne Bell.
Description: Springville, Utah : Front Table Books, An imprint of Cedar Fort, Inc., [2018]
Identifiers: LCCN 2017042685 | ISBN 9781462121540 (hardcover : alk. paper)
Subjects: LCSH: Cooking (Popcorn) | LCGFT: Cookbooks.
Classification: LCC TX814.5.P66 B45 2018 | DDC 641.6/5677--dc23
LC record available at https://lccn.loc.gov/2017042685

Cover and page design by Katie Payne
Cover design © 2018 Cedar Fort, Inc.
Edited by Melissa Caldwell and Erica Myers

Printed in Korea
10 9 8 7 6 5 4 3 2 1

Printed on acid-free paper

For my summer assistants—Rachel, Evy, and Amelia

WHITE POPCORN

ALMOND BARK

YELLOW POPCORN

MELTING WAFERS

MUSHROOM POPCORN

CONTENTS

INTRODUCTION

I'm a little bit obsessed with popcorn. Really though, what's not to love? It's light. It's crunchy. It can be sweet. It can be savory. Kids love it. Adults love it. And best of all—it's FAST and EASY. Also, when you consider this snack was probably discovered by accident, it's safe to assume it's not going to be judging you. By nature, popcorn recipes are usually quite forgiving. You have a little more chocolate? Add a little more chocolate. Don't have quite enough butter? Use a little less. Popcorn is the perfect low-stress snack to satisfy all of your cravings!

I hope you enjoy the recipes in this book and that they inspire you to put popcorn on the snack menu at your house!

COOKING TIPS

POPPING METHODS

Popcorn has been around for centuries. Luckily for us, popping methods have only gotten better with time. We no longer have to rely on fire to make popcorn. In today's world, we have a variety of methods to pop our popcorn. The best popping method for you might be different than the best method for someone else. Pick a method that doesn't seem like a chore and get to making that delicious popcorn!

Air Popper – Hot air popcorn poppers have come a long way in the last few decades. They are quicker and more efficient than they've ever been. Air poppers are available at most large retail stores and online. They are simple to use and make popcorn that is completely free of any other flavor. Generally, a popper is plugged in and/or turned on. Popcorn kernels are poured in and pop as they are heated. The moving air shoots them out of the tunnel and into the bowl you have ready and waiting. As always, you should follow the manufacturer's instructions for any appliance. One-half cup kernels makes 10–12 cups popped popcorn.

Stovetop – Making popcorn on a stovetop requires no special equipment other than a 3- to 4-quart pot with a lid. Place the pot on a stovetop and pour in 3 tablespoons of oil. Be sure to use oil with a high smoke point such as peanut or canola oil. Drop 3 kernels into the pot. Place the lid on top. If the lid has a vent, open it to allow steam to escape. Heat the pot on medium-high heat. Listen for the kernels to pop. When they have all popped, quickly pour in ½ cup of popcorn kernels. Replace the lid and shake the pot back and forth to coat the kernels with oil. The pot will be very hot! Please protect your hands. Once the popping starts, gently shake the pot back and forth over the burner. When the popping slows, remove from heat and pour into a serving bowl.

This is my favorite method. It can be salted immediately and eaten without any other flavoring. The oil also leaves a very thin protective layer on the popcorn, which allows it to hold up to some of the more liquid or sticky recipes in this book. One-half cup kernels makes 10–12 cups popped popcorn.

Microwave – Did you know that fresh popcorn can also be made in a microwave? You can use either a paper bag or glass bowl to make popcorn in your microwave without any added flavors or chemicals.

Paper Bag – Open a lunch-size paper bag. Pour ¼ cup popcorn kernels into the bag. Fold the top down three times, leaving space for the popcorn to pop into. Place horizontally in a microwave. Microwave at full power for 3–5 minutes. Stay near the microwave and remove when popping slows. One-quarter cup kernels make 4–5 cups popped popcorn.

Glass Bowl – Place ¼ cup popcorn kernels in a microwave-safe glass bowl that will hold at least 8 cups. Place a microwave-safe plate on top. It's best if the plate isn't a perfect match so steam can escape. Microwave at full power for 4–6 minutes. Stay near the microwave and remove when popping slows. Be very careful! The glass bowl will be HOT! While this method isn't as efficient as the previous two methods, it is my children's favorite way to make popcorn because they can watch it pop through a clear glass bowl. One-quarter cup kernels make 4–5 cups popped popcorn.

Single-Use Microwave Popcorn Bags – I prefer the light taste of all the previous popping methods. But let's be honest -- sometimes those microwave popcorn bags from the store are what you have. For best results, gently knead the popcorn bags before placing them in the microwave. Microwave on full power for 3–5 minutes. Stay near the microwave and remove when popping slows. When making recipes in this book, choose flavors such as "light" or "natural" to minimize butter flavor interference. A 3.2-ounce bag of popcorn makes about 10 cups of popped popcorn.

INGREDIENTS
Unlike many other delicious gourmet treats, popcorn doesn't require hard-

to-find ingredients that cost as much as your monthly rent. Sometimes the simplest of ingredients can be combined in the most delicious ways. This is certainly true of an unpresuming snack like popcorn. Most ingredients from this book can be purchased easily from your local grocery store. A few ingredients, such as the popcorn kernels themselves and the melting chocolate, while still easily accessible, require just a little more thought before purchasing.

Popcorn Kernels – There are 4 major types of popcorn kernels: White, yellow, flint, and mushroom. White and yellow kernels are commonly sold in grocery stores across the nation. When popped, white kernels are small and have a bright white color. Yellow kernels are a bit larger and have a creamy, ivory color. Flint corn kernels are more of a novelty. The popped corn is white in color like white kernels, but is even smaller in size. White, yellow, and flint kernels all pop in a butterfly shape. That is, the popped corn seems to have two flattish sides. Mushroom kernels, on the other hand, are large and round when popped. Mushroom kernels can be found at some specialty food

stores or online. Mushroom kernels are my favorite for popcorn recipes that use chocolate, syrup, or liquid, as the stronger structure makes them more capable of withstanding stirring or saturation. The delicate, crisp structure of the white and yellow kernels lends itself well to popcorn flavored with powders or fresh herbs.

Popcorn kernels have a very precise ideal moisture content: 13.5–14 percent. Too much or not enough moisture will result in more unpopped kernels or partially popped kernels. Popcorn should be stored in an airtight container away from steam or heat.

Melting Chocolate – Recipes in this book that use chocolate call for "melting chocolate." Real chocolate requires tempering when melted so that it will harden correctly. While it tastes amazing, it can also be a little demanding. Melting chocolate, or chocolate candy coating, is made with different fats that make melting, pouring, and mixing easier. The two most common and widely available forms of melting chocolate are melting wafers and almond bark.

Melting Wafers – Also known as candy coating, compound coating, or candy melts, these look like round little buttons of chocolate. They could not be easier to use. Simply pour them into a glass bowl and microwave. Stir at 30-second intervals until thin and smooth. Melting wafers come in many flavors and colors.

Almond Bark – Generally found in the baking aisle of most grocery stores, almond bark comes in chocolate and white chocolate options. It looks like a giant candy bar with indentations to mark 1- or 2-ounce sections of the melting chocolate. Since the lines are clearly marked, it is easy to measure. Use a large knife to chop off the amount of melting chocolate that you need. Chop into smaller pieces and pour into a glass bowl. Microwave for 30 seconds at a time, then stir. Continue stirring and microwaving until thin and smooth.

Chocolate Chips – In a pinch, chocolate chips can be used. Chocolate chips, however, are made with different fats that are designed to hold their shape. You could throw a handful of chocolate chips onto a baking sheet and place it a hot oven for ten minutes. When you take the baking sheet out, the chocolate chips may not even look melted, but will flatten when touched. Pour the desired amount of chocolate chips into a glass bowl and microwave for 30 seconds at a time. Be sure to stir each time, as chocolate chips can burn before you realize they are even melted.

STORING AND PACKAGING
Always allow popcorn to cool or dry completely before storing. Place popcorn in an airtight container and store in a cool, dry place. Popcorn makes an excellent gift. You can find self-sealing cellophane bags online in large sizes for entire batches of popcorn. The self-sealing tape at the edge creates an airtight seal to keep the popcorn tasting fresh. Greaseproof or wax-lined bags and cups are a more festive option for storing and sharing popcorn. Place these visually attractive package options inside a clear cellophane bag or other airtight container if storing for more then 24 hours.

POPCORN FOR A CROWD
Popcorn is the PERFECT snack for large groups! You can prepare it in

minutes instead of hours or days. Many of the recipes in this book can be made days ahead of the big event. Less time in the kitchen means more time for other party preparations. If you've never served popcorn at a large gathering, use these helpful tips to get you started.

Plan on about 4 cups of prepared popcorn per person if popcorn is the only food item. For example, at a backyard movie or for game night.

Plan on about 2 cups of prepared popcorn per person if other food items will be served.

Include both sweet and savory popcorns on your menu. The combination of sweet and salty keeps things interesting for our taste buds.

For most popcorns, a tall, deep bowl is best for serving. Popcorn is more difficult to serve out of wide, shallow bowls.

Be prepared with scoops! In a pinch, you can use 1-cup measuring spoons or ladles to serve the popcorn. Paper cups are another, more casual option, both for serving and to hold the popcorn.

For chewy or sticky recipes, consider pulling balls of popcorn apart and placing them on a plate so guests can easily grab a small amount of popcorn without touching the entire batch of popcorn.

Don't forget the drinks! Popcorn makes everyone thirsty.

TIPS FOR SUCCESS

Use the stovetop popping method for popping popcorn that will be used in wet or sticky recipes.

Pop in small batches to avoid burning or popcorn bursting out of the container.

When separating unpopped or partially popped kernels from the popped popcorn, place the popcorn in a bag or bowl. Shake a few times. The heavier kernels and partially popped kernels will fall to the bottom. Gently remove the popped popcorn from the top and place in another bowl.

Use a larger bowl than you think you will need. It always helps to have a little more space for stirring.

SWEET

BANANA BREAD

INGREDIENTS:

10–12 cups popped popcorn
1/2 cup unsalted butter
1/2 cup brown sugar
1 tsp. vanilla
2 tsp. banana flavoring

1 tsp. cinnamon
1/2 tsp. allspice
1/8 tsp. salt
1/2 cup chopped walnuts
1 cup mini chocolate chips
1 cup banana chips

The smell of banana bread baking in the oven is easily one of my children's favorite smells, but it can be so hard for them to wait! Now they can have all the same delicious flavors in just minutes!

1. Place popcorn in a large bowl. Remove any unpopped or partially popped kernels.

2. Place butter in a microwave safe bowl and cover with a paper towel. Microwave for 30 seconds at a time until melted. Add brown sugar, vanilla, banana flavoring, cinnamon, allspice, and salt. Mix well. Pour over popcorn and stir to coat. Add walnuts, chocolate chips, and banana chips. Stir again. Store in an airtight container for up to one week.

BANANA SPLIT

INGREDIENTS:

10–12 cups popped popcorn
¾ cup sugar
¼ cup corn syrup
2 Tbsp. unsalted butter
½ tsp. baking soda
2 tsp. banana flavoring

4 oz. melting chocolate
1 cup mini marshmallows
1 cup banana chips
¼ cup sprinkles

This recipe has all the best parts of an ice cream sundae: the toppings! When combined with the surprising crunch of the banana layer, this popcorn is hard to resist!

1. Place popcorn in a large bowl. Remove any unpopped or partially popped kernels.

2. In a medium saucepan, stir together sugar and corn syrup. Add butter and heat on medium high, stirring occasionally. When the mixture comes to a boil, allow to boil for three minutes without stirring. Remove from heat and immediately add baking soda and banana flavoring. Stir to combine. The mixture will be foamy. Pour over popcorn while still hot. Stir gently until the popcorn is completely coated. Spread on a parchment-lined baking sheet. Break apart when cool.

3. Place melting chocolate in a microwave-safe bowl. Microwave for 30 seconds at a time, stirring in between, until completely melted. Drizzle over popcorn. Immediately sprinkle with marshmallows, banana chips and sprinkles. Allow to cool. Store in an airtight container for up to one week.

BIRTHDAY CAKE

Birthday cake popcorn is the perfect way to celebrate when you are in a rush! There's no need for forks and napkins, and there is no icing to get smooshed. Serve birthday cake popcorn for a fun and surprising change! Try different flavors of cake mix for even more fun flavors.

INGREDIENTS:

10–12 cups popped popcorn
6 oz. white melting chocolate
1 cup white cake mix

¼ cup sprinkles

1. Place popcorn in a large bowl. Remove any unpopped or partially popped kernels.

2. Place melting chocolate in a microwave safe bowl. Microwave for 30 seconds at a time, stirring in between, until completely melted. Pour over popcorn and stir to coat. Sprinkle cake mix over popcorn and stir again. Add sprinkles and stir to evenly distribute. Store in an airtight container for up to one week.

BLUEBERRIES AND CREAM

This soft and gooey blueberry popcorn will have you convinced that it needs to be eaten for breakfast. And lunch. And dinner. If you want even more blueberry flavor, you can add fresh blueberries to the popcorn just before spreading the popcorn on a baking sheet. Serve as soon as the popcorn is cool if you choose to do so.

INGREDIENTS:

10–12 cups popped popcorn   6 oz. white melting chocolate
1/2 cup granulated sugar
2/3 cup blueberry syrup
1 Tbsp. butter

1. Place popcorn in a large bowl. Remove any unpopped or partially popped kernels.

2. In a medium saucepan, stir together sugar and syrup. Add butter and heat on medium high, stirring occasionally. When the mixture comes to a boil, allow to boil for four minutes without stirring. Remove from heat. Pour over popcorn. Stir gently until the popcorn is completely coated. Spread on parchment lined baking sheet.

3. Place melting chocolate in a microwave safe bowl. Microwave for 30 seconds at a time, stirring in between, until completely melted. Drizzle over popcorn and stir to coat. Store in an airtight container for up to one week.

BROWNIE

INGREDIENTS:

10–12 cups popped popcorn
6 oz. melting chocolate
1 cup powdered brownie mix

Brownie popcorn could NOT be easier. It's quick to make and impossible to stop eating. Make it today and it will soon be one of your favorites!

1. Place popcorn in a large bowl. Remove any unpopped or partially popped kernels.

2. Place melting chocolate in a microwave safe bowl. Microwave for 30 seconds at a time, stirring in between, until completely melted. Pour over popcorn and stir to coat. Sprinkle brownie mix over the popcorn and stir to coat. Store in an airtight container for up to a week.

INGREDIENTS:

10–12 cups popped popcorn
1 cup pecans
1/3 cup granulated sugar
2 Tbsp. unsalted butter
6 Tbsp. unsalted butter

1/3 cup brown sugar
1 tsp. vanilla

This is a great recipe to make for a social gathering. The amazing aroma from the pecans cooking in the butter and sugar will make everyone instantly hungry when they walk through your door!

1. Place popcorn in a large bowl. Remove any unpopped or partially popped kernels.

2. Heat pecans in a large frying pan on medium heat until aromatic (about 2–3 minutes). Add granulated sugar and 2 tablespoons butter. Cook 2 more minutes, or until the sugar starts to turn a golden color. Spread to cool on a piece of parchment.

3. Place 6 tablespoons butter in a microwave safe bowl and cover with a paper towel. Microwave for 30 seconds at a time until melted. Add brown sugar and vanilla. Mix well. Pour over popcorn and stir to coat. Add butter pecans and stir to evenly distribute. Store in an airtight container for up to one week.

BUTTER PECAN

BUTTERSCOTCH

INGREDIENTS:

10–12 cups popped popcorn

1/2 cup butterscotch ice cream syrup

2/3 cup granulated sugar

1 Tbsp. unsalted butter

1/2 tsp. baking soda

1 tsp. vanilla

Butterscotch is making a comeback! This perfectly chewy butterscotch popcorn has a light, fresh flavor that kids and grandparents will love!

1. Place popcorn in a large bowl. Remove any unpopped or partially popped kernels.

2. In a medium saucepan, stir together syrup and sugar. Add butter and heat on medium high, stirring occasionally. When the mixture comes to a boil, allow to boil for 3 minutes without stirring. Remove from heat and immediately add baking soda and vanilla. Stir to combine. Pour over popcorn while still hot. Stir gently until the popcorn is completely coated.

CANDY BAR

INGREDIENTS:

10–12 cups popped popcorn
1 cup peanuts
2 cups mini marshmallows
1½ cups caramel bits (11-oz. package)
4 tsp. water
6 oz. melting chocolate

All of your favorite candy bar ingredients come together in this recipe of goodness and decadence! You could also add pretzels, malt powder, or chocolate chips if you want to get even crazier.

1. Place popcorn in a large bowl. Remove any unpopped or partially popped kernels. Add peanuts and marshmallows and stir to evenly distribute.

2. Place caramel and water in a microwave safe bowl. Microwave for 30 seconds and stir. Repeat until completely melted and smooth. Pour over popcorn and stir to coat. Spread on parchment lined baking sheet to cool.

3. Place melting chocolate in a microwave safe bowl. Microwave for 30 seconds at a time and stir. Repeat until completely melted. Drizzle over popcorn and allow to cool. Store in an airtight container for up to one week.

CANDY COATING

Try these fun flavor combinations!

- **Banana Cream Pie** – 1 tsp. vanilla and 1 tsp. banana flavoring
- **Butter Rum** – 1 tsp. butter flavoring and 1 tsp. rum flavoring
- **Coconut Cream** – 1 tsp. vanilla and 1 tsp. coconut flavoring
- **Fruit Punch** – 1 tsp. cherry flavoring, 1 tsp orange flavoring, and 1 tsp lemon flavoring
- **Fuzzy Navel** – 1 tsp. orange flavoring and 1 tsp. peach flavoring
- **Hawaiian Punch** -- 1 tsp. strawberry flavoring, 1 tsp. pineapple flavoring, and 1 tsp. vanilla
- **Mai Tai** – 1 tsp. pineapple flavoring, 1 tsp. lemon flavoring, and 1 tsp. orange flavoring
- **Mixed Berry** – 1 tsp. strawberry flavoring, 1 tsp. cherry flavoring, and 1 tsp. raspberry flavoring
- **Peach Razzmatazz** – 1 tsp. peach flavoring and 1 tsp. raspberry flavoring
- **Pina Colada** – 1 tsp. coconut flavoring and 1 tsp. pineapple flavoring
- **Strawberry Banana** – 1 tsp. strawberry flavoring and 1 tsp. banana flavoring
- **Strawberry Cheesecake** – 1 tsp. strawberry flavoring and 1 tsp. cheesecake flavoring
- **Strawberry Daiquiri** – 1 tsp. strawberry flavoring and 1 tsp. pineapple flavoring
- **Tiger's Blood** – 1 tsp. coconut flavoring and 1 tsp. strawberry flavoring
- **Wedding Cake** – 1sp. vanilla and 1 tsp. almond flavoring

INGREDIENTS:

10–12 cups popped popcorn
1 cup granulated sugar
½ cup water

1 Tbsp. unsalted butter
½ tsp. baking soda
2 tsp. flavoring of your choice

1. Place popcorn in a large bowl. Remove any unpopped or partially popped kernels.

2. In a medium saucepan, stir together sugar and water. Add butter and heat on medium high, stirring occasionally. When the mixture comes to a boil, allow to boil for 3 minutes without stirring. Remove from heat and immediately add baking soda and flavoring. Stir to combine. The mixture will be foamy. Pour over popcorn while still hot. Stir gently until the popcorn is completely coated. Allow to cool before serving.

INGREDIENTS:

10–12 cups popped popcorn
1 cup shredded coconut
1½ cups caramel bits (about 11 oz.)
4 tsp. water
4 oz. melting chocolate

Just like the popular caramel coconut cookies, this popcorn won't last long once you've taken that first bite! Add an extra cup of shredded coconut if you just can't get enough coconut in your life.

1. Place popcorn in a large bowl. Remove any unpopped or partially popped kernels. Add shredded coconut and stir to evenly distribute.

2. Place caramel and water in a microwave safe bowl. Microwave for 30 seconds and stir. Repeat until completely melted and smooth. Pour over popcorn and stir to coat. Spread on parchment lined baking sheet to cool.

3. Place melting chocolate in a microwave safe bowl. Microwave for 30 seconds at a time and stir. Repeat until completely melted. Drizzle over popcorn. Allow to cool. Store in an airtight container for up to one week.

CARAMEL COCONUT FUDGE

CHERRY CHOCOLATE

INGREDIENTS:

10–12 cups popped popcorn

6 oz. melting chocolate

1 cup chopped cherry sour candies
(about 8 oz.)

The sweet, tart flavor from the cherry candies in this recipe is the perfect contrast to the mellow chocolate flavor. Rub a little cooking oil on your knife before cutting the candies to keep the cherry candies from sticking to your knife.

1. Place popcorn in a large bowl. Remove any unpopped or partially popped kernels.

2. Place melting chocolate in a microwave safe bowl. Microwave for 30 seconds at a time. Stir and repeat until completely melted. Pour over popcorn and stir to coat. Add chopped cherry candies and stir to distribute evenly. Allow to cool. Store in an airtight container for up to one week.

CHERRY TURNOVER

This cherry turnover popcorn is easier to make than the real thing but will still have your taste buds screaming for more! Double the amount of cherry candies if you want to increase the sweet and tart factor.

INGREDIENTS:

10–12 cups popped popcorn
½ cup unsalted butter
½ cup granulated sugar
¼ cup flour
¼ tsp. salt

1 tsp. vanilla
1 cup powdered sugar
1 cup chopped cherry sour candies

1. Place popcorn in a large bowl. Remove any unpopped or partially popped kernels.

2. Place butter in a microwave safe bowl and cover with a paper towel. Microwave for 30 seconds at a time until melted. Add sugar, flour, salt, and vanilla. Mix well. Pour over popcorn and stir to coat. Sprinkle powdered sugar on top and stir to combine. Mix in chopped cherry candies. Store in an airtight container for up to one week.

CHEWY CARAMEL CORN

Soft and gooey caramel popcorn is a timeless favorite! The sweetened condensed milk gives this popcorn a thick, creamy texture that is guaranteed to make the popcorn disappear. Go ahead and make a double batch—this recipe doubles well!

INGREDIENTS:

10–12 cups popped popcorn
½ cup unsalted butter
1 cup brown sugar
½ cup corn syrup
½ cup sweetened condensed milk
½ tsp. salt
1 tsp. vanilla

1. Place popcorn in a large bowl. Remove any unpopped or partially popped kernels.

2. Place butter, brown sugar, and corn syrup in a medium saucepan. Mix well. Heat on medium-high heat until boiling. Add sweetened condensed milk and return to a boil. Boil for 4 minutes, stirring constantly. (The mixture should be about 234° F or softball stage.) Remove from heat. Add salt and vanilla and mix well. Pour over popcorn and stir to coat. Allow to cool. Store in an airtight container for up to one week.

CHOCOLATE CARAMEL PRETZEL

The soft caramel and crunchy pretzels in this recipe are a winning combination! Reminiscent of gourmet pretzel rods, this just might become your new favorite way to eat popcorn!

INGREDIENTS:

10–12 cups popped popcorn

1½ cups broken pretzel pieces

1½ cups caramel bits (about 11 oz.)

1½ Tbsp. water

4 oz. melting chocolate

1. Place popcorn on a parchment lined baking sheet. Remove any unpopped or partially popped kernels. Add pretzel pieces.

2. Place caramel bits and water in a microwave safe bowl. Microwave for 30 seconds and stir. Repeat until melted and smooth. Drizzle over popcorn.

3. Place melting chocolate in a microwave safe bowl. Microwave for 30 seconds and stir. Repeat until completely melted. Drizzle over popcorn. Store in an airtight container for up to one week.

CHOCOLATE CHIP COOKIE DOUGH

Everybody's favorite flavor meets everybody's favorite snack! But don't let the kids have all the fun— Chocolate Chip Cookie Dough Popcorn is a favorite of adults too!

INGREDIENTS:

10–12 cups popped popcorn
1/2 cup unsalted butter
2/3 cup brown sugar
1/3 cup flour
1/4 tsp. salt

1 tsp. vanilla
1/2 cup mini chocolate chips

1. Place popcorn in a large bowl. Remove any unpopped or partially popped kernels.

2. Place butter in a microwave safe bowl and cover with a paper towel. Microwave for 30 seconds at a time until melted. Add brown sugar, flour, salt, and vanilla. Mix well. Pour over popcorn and stir to coat. Add chocolate chips and stir again. Store in an airtight container for up to one week.

CHURRO

INGREDIENTS:
10–12 cups popped popcorn
½ cup unsalted butter
¼ cup flour
½ cup granulated sugar, divided
2 tsp. cinnamon, divided

You no longer have to wait for the summer carnival for your favorite fried pastry flavor! Try adding toasted cinnamon cereal pieces or cinnamon chips for extra flavor and crunch.

1. Place popcorn in a large bowl. Remove any unpopped or partially popped kernels.

2. Place butter in a microwave safe bowl and cover with a paper towel. Microwave for 30 seconds at a time until melted. Add flour, ¼ cup sugar, and 1 tsp. cinnamon. Stir until well blended. Pour over popcorn and stir to coat. Mix remaining ¼ cup sugar and 1 tsp. cinnamon together and sprinkle over the top of the popcorn. Store in an airtight container for up to one week.

CINNAMON HOT

INGREDIENTS:
10–12 cups popped popcorn
1 cup cinnamon candies (about 8 oz.)
2 Tbsp. water

My mother shared this recipe with me. She likes to make smaller batches at a time to enjoy by herself. Be aware—the cinnamon candies cool and set up very quickly. Be ready stir as soon as you pour the melted candies over the popcorn.

1. Place popcorn in a large bowl. Remove any unpopped or partially popped kernels.

2. Place candies and water in a microwave safe bowl and cover with a paper towel. Microwave for 60 seconds and stir. Continue melting at 30 second intervals until melted and smooth. Immediately pour over popcorn and stir quickly to coat. Spread on baking sheet to cool. Store in an airtight container for up to one week.

CINNAMON ROLL

There couldn't be a popcorn recipe better suited for Saturday morning cartoons. Make this popcorn for your loved ones on cool mornings and enjoy a little extra cuddle time.

INGREDIENTS:

10–12 cups popped popcorn
½ cup unsalted butter
¼ cup granulated sugar
2 tsp. cinnamon
¼ cup unsalted butter

4 oz. cream cheese
½ tsp. vanilla

1. Place popcorn in a large bowl. Remove any unpopped or partially popped kernels.

2. Place ½ cup butter in a microwave safe bowl and cover with a paper towel. Microwave for 30 seconds at a time until melted. Add sugar and cinnamon. Mix well. Pour over popcorn and stir to coat. Spread on parchment lined baking sheet.

3. Place ¼ cup butter and cream cheese in a microwave safe bowl and cover with a paper towel. Microwave for 30 seconds at a time until melted. Add vanilla and mix well. Drizzle over popcorn. Serve immediately.

COFFEE CAKE

INGREDIENTS:

10–12 cups popped
popcorn
¼ cup butter
¼ cup flour
½ cup sugar
1 tsp. cinnamon

1 cup sugar
¼ cup water
1 Tbsp. butter
½ tsp. baking soda
2 tsp. butter flavoring
1 tsp. vanilla flavoring

Say hello to morning with a big bowl of delicious coffee cake popcorn. It's a perfect companion to any warm beverage of your choice.

1. Place popcorn in a large bowl. Remove any unpopped or partially popped kernels.

2. In a small bowl, cut together ¼ cup butter, ¼ cup flour, ½ cup sugar, and cinnamon until it resembles coarse crumbs. Set aside.

3. In a medium saucepan, stir together 1 cup sugar and water. Add 1 tablespoon butter and heat on medium high, stirring occasionally. When the mixture comes to a boil, allow to boil for 3 minutes without stirring. Remove from heat and immediately add baking soda and flavorings. Stir to combine. The mixture will be foamy. Pour over popcorn while still hot. Stir gently until the popcorn is completely coated. Add crumb mixture and stir again. Allow to cool. Store in an airtight container for up to one week.

INGREDIENTS:

10–12 cups popped popcorn

6 oz. white melting chocolate

1½ cup crumbled chocolate sandwich cookies (about 15 cookies)

You really can have it all—in one bowl! No more deciding between popcorn and chocolate sandwich cookies. This Cookies and Cream Popcorn is sure to be a favorite!

1. Place popcorn in a large bowl. Remove any unpopped or partially popped kernels.

2. Place melting chocolate in a microwave safe bowl. Microwave for 30 seconds at a time and stir. Repeat until completely melted. Pour over popcorn and stir to coat. Add crumbled sandwich cookies and stir again. Store in an airtight container for up to one week.

COOKIES AND CREAM

The creamy cinnamon chips and chewy apple slices are a winning combination! I was concerned that apple slices would be difficult to find, but I saw them in multiple grocery stores. They are generally found on the top shelf above where raisins are sold.

INGREDIENTS:

10–12 cups popcorn
¼ cup granulated sugar
1 tsp. cinnamon
1 cup cinnamon chips

2 cups chopped dried apple slices

1. Place popcorn in a large bowl. Remove any unpopped or partially popped kernels.

2. In a small bowl, combine sugar and cinnamon. Set aside.

3. Place cinnamon chips in a microwave safe bowl. Microwave for 30 seconds at a time and stir. Repeat until completely melted. Pour over popcorn and stir to coat. Add chopped apple slices and stir again. Sprinkle with cinnamon sugar mixture. Store in an airtight container for up to one week.

COUNTRY APPLE PIE

CRUNCHY CARAMEL CORN

It really doesn't get any better than this. Crunchy caramel corn is a longtime national favorite. Mix some of this Crunchy Caramel Corn with the Three Cheese Popcorn for your very own Chicago Mix Popcorn.

INGREDIENTS:

10–12 cups popped popcorn
½ cup unsalted butter
1 cup brown sugar
¼ cup corn syrup

½ tsp. salt
¼ tsp. baking soda
1 tsp. vanilla

1. Preheat oven to 250°F.

2. Place popcorn in a large bowl. Remove any unpopped or partially popped kernels.

3. In a medium saucepan, stir together butter, brown sugar, and corn syrup. Heat on medium high, stirring occasionally. When the mixture comes to a boil, allow to boil for 4 minutes without stirring. Remove from heat and immediately add salt, baking soda, and vanilla. Stir to combine. The mixture will be foamy. Pour over popcorn while still hot. Stir gently until the popcorn is completely coated.

4. Spread on parchment lined baking sheet and bake for 30 minutes. Stir after 15 minutes. Leave on baking sheet until cool. Store in an airtight container for up to one week.

33

FLUFFERNUTTER

This delightfully tasty combination of peanut butter and marshmallow is sure to be a hit with peanut butter lovers everywhere! Try adding additional marshmallows to the cooled popcorn for even more "fluff" flavor.

INGREDIENTS:

10–12 cups popped popcorn
½ cup unsalted butter
½ cup peanut butter
2 cups mini marshmallows
½ cup chocolate chips

1. Place popcorn in a large bowl. Remove any unpopped or partially popped kernels.

2. Place butter and peanut butter in a microwave safe bowl and cover with a paper towel. Microwave for 30 seconds at a time until melted. Pour over popcorn and stir to coat. Immediately add marshmallows and stir again. Marshmallows will melt into the peanut butter mixture as you stir. Add chocolate chips when the popcorn has cooled slightly. Store in an airtight container for up to one week.

INGREDIENTS:

10–12 cups popped popcorn
2/3 cup granulated sugar
1/2 cup maple syrup
1 Tbsp. unsalted butter

1 tsp. cinnamon
1 Tbsp. vanilla
1/2 tsp. baking soda

Wake up with this soft and gooey French Toast Popcorn recipe. Serve it with orange juice and fresh fruit for a full breakfast flavor profile!

1. Place popcorn in a large bowl. Remove any unpopped or partially popped kernels.

2. In a medium saucepan, stir together sugar and maple syrup. Add butter and heat on medium high, stirring occasionally. When the mixture comes to a boil, allow to boil for 4 minutes without stirring. Remove from heat and immediately add cinnamon, vanilla, and baking soda. Stir to combine. Pour over popcorn while still hot. Stir gently until the popcorn is completely coated. Allow to cool. Store in an airtight container for up to one week.

FRENCH TOAST

FRENCH VANILLA

INGREDIENTS:

10–12 cups popped popcorn
6 oz. white melting chocolate
1 box (3.5 oz.) french vanilla pudding mix

Simple and classy, french vanilla flavor never goes out of style! It's the perfect choice for even the pickiest of eaters.

1. Place popcorn in a large bowl. Remove any unpopped or partially popped kernels.
2. Place melting chocolate in a microwave safe bowl. Microwave for 30 seconds at a time, then stir. Repeat until completely melted. Pour over popcorn and stir to coat. Sprinkle pudding mix over popcorn and stir to evenly distribute. Allow to cool. Store in an airtight container for up to one week.

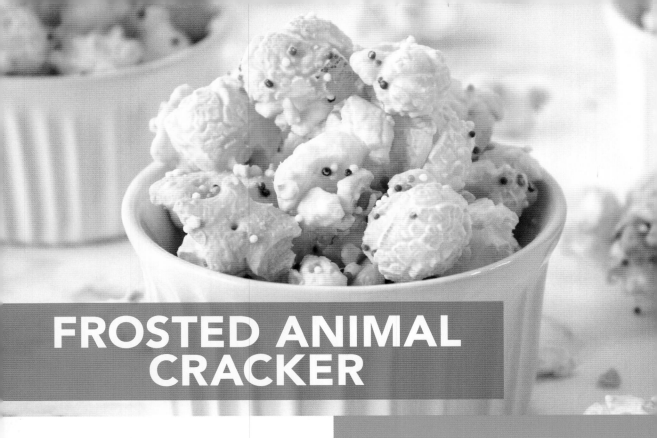

FROSTED ANIMAL CRACKER

INGREDIENTS:

10–12 cups popped popcorn

2 cups animal crackers

6 oz. pink melting chocolate (about 1 cup melting wafers)

2 Tbsp. nonpareils

Bring back the nostalgia with this pink and white Frosted Animal Crackers Popcorn! Pink melting chocolate can sometimes be found in the baking aisle at the grocery store or in the cake aisle at craft stores.

1. Place popcorn in a large bowl. Remove any unpopped or partially popped kernels. Add animal crackers to the bowl.

2. Place melting chocolate in a microwave safe bowl. Microwave for 30 seconds at a time, then stir. Repeat until completely melted. Pour over popcorn and stir to coat. Add nonpareils and stir again. Store in an airtight container for up to one week.

FROSTED FRIENDS

INGREDIENTS:

10–12 cups popped popcorn
½ cup unsalted butter
½ cup creamy peanut butter
6 oz melting chocolate
2 cups powdered sugar

Try adding peanuts or chocolate candies to the mix! This also tastes amazing when stored in the freezer!

1. Place popcorn in a large bowl. Remove any unpopped or partially popped kernels.

2. Place butter, peanut butter, and melting chocolate in a microwave safe bowl and cover with a paper towel. Microwave for 30 seconds at a time, stirring in between, until melted and smooth. Pour over popcorn and stir to coat. Sprinkle powdered sugar over popcorn and gently stir until evenly distributed. Spread on baking sheet to cool. Store in an airtight container for up to one week.

FUDGE

With only two
ingredients,
this Fudge
Popcorn
could NOT
be easier! Try
using different
flavors of
premade
frosting
to make
different kinds
of Fudge
Popcorn!

INGREDIENTS:

10–12 cups popped popcorn
4 oz. melting chocolate
1 cup premade chocolate frosting

....

1. Place popcorn in a large bowl. Remove any unpopped or partially popped kernels.

2. Place melting chocolate and frosting in a microwave safe bowl. Microwave for 30 seconds at a time, stirring in between, until completely melted. Pour over popcorn and stir to coat. Allow to cool. Store in an airtight container for up to one week.

INGREDIENTS:

10–12 cups popped popcorn
½ cup dried coconut
½ cup chopped pecans
½ cup unsalted butter
½ cup brown sugar

½ cup unsalted butter
2 Tbsp. unsweetened cocoa powder
1 cup powdered sugar
½ tsp. vanilla

1. Place popcorn in a large bowl. Remove any unpopped or partially popped kernels. Add coconut and pecans and stir to evenly distribute.

2. Place ½ cup butter in a microwave safe bowl and cover with a paper towel. Microwave for 30 seconds at a time until melted. Add brown sugar and mix well. Pour over popcorn and stir to coat. Spread on parchment lined baking sheet to cool.

3. Place ½ cup butter in a microwave safe bowl and cover with a paper towel. Microwave for 30 seconds at a time until melted. Add cocoa powder, powdered sugar, and vanilla. Mix well. Drizzle over popcorn and allow to cool. Store in an airtight container for up to one week.

GERMAN CHOCOLATE

GINGERBREAD

INGREDIENTS:

10–12 cups popped popcorn
1/2 cup unsalted butter
1/3 cup molasses
1/3 cup brown sugar
1/4 cup flour

1 tsp. cinnamon
1/2 tsp. ground ginger
1/2 tsp. allspice

Gingerbread is traditionally a winter holiday flavor and would make an excellent gift . . . but why not be adventurous and try it year-round?

1. Place popcorn in a large bowl. Remove any unpopped or partially popped kernels.

2. Place butter and molasses in a microwave safe bowl and cover with a paper towel. Microwave for 30 seconds at a time until melted. Add brown sugar, flour, cinnamon, ginger, and allspice. Mix well. Pour over popcorn and stir to coat. Allow to cool. Store in an airtight container for up to one week.

INGREDIENTS:

10–12 cups popped popcorn
1/2 cup unsalted butter
1/3 cup honey
1/4 cup brown sugar
1/2 tsp. cinnamon
1/2 tsp. nutmeg
1/4 tsp. salt

1 1/2 cups rolled oats
2 cups total of the following: dried cranberries, raisins, pumpkin seeds, slivered almonds, and sunflower seeds

Fully customizable, this healthy Granola Popcorn is made to order! Fill it with all your favorites and make extra for a perfect after-school snack!

1. Place popcorn in a large bowl. Remove any unpopped or partially popped kernels.

2. Place butter in a microwave safe bowl and cover with a paper towel. Microwave for 30 seconds at a time until melted. Add honey, brown sugar, cinnamon, nutmeg, and salt. Mix well. Drizzle over popcorn and stir to coat. Add oats and berry-nut mixture. Stir again to combine. Allow to cool. Store in an airtight container for up to one week.

GRANOLA

INGREDIENTS:

10–12 cups popped popcorn
½ cup unsalted butter
1 cup hazelnut spread
¼ cup powdered sugar
¼ tsp. salt

The popular hazelnut and chocolate combo make this Hazelnut Popcorn impossible to resist! If the butter and spread mixture is a little thick, try microwaving them together for an additional 10 seconds.

1. Place popcorn in a large bowl. Remove any unpopped or partially popped kernels.

2. Place butter in a microwave safe bowl and cover with a paper towel. Microwave for 30 seconds at a time until melted. Add hazelnut spread, powdered sugar, and salt. Mix well. Immediately pour over popcorn and stir to coat. Allow to cool. Store in an airtight container for up to one week.

HAZELNUT

HONEY BUTTER

INGREDIENTS:
10–12 cups popped popcorn
1/2 cup unsalted butter
1/3 cup honey

The light flavor of this Honey Butter Popcorn is the perfect mix of sweet and salty. Try adding 1/2 teaspoon of cinnamon for a subtle surprise!

1. Place popcorn in a large bowl. Remove any unpopped or partially popped kernels.

2. Place butter in a microwave safe bowl and cover with a paper towel. Microwave for 30 seconds at a time until melted. Add honey and mix well. Pour over popcorn and stir to coat. Allow to cool. Store in an airtight container for up to one week.

HONEY NUT

INGREDIENTS:

10–12 cups popped popcorn
1/2 cup unsalted butter
1/4 cup creamy peanut butter
1/3 cup honey
1 cup peanuts

When I was growing up, we only had "healthy" cereals at my house. Honey Nut was my absolute favorite because it was as close to sugar as I was ever going to get! It's still one of my favorites as an adult, and although I now eat a ridiculous amount of sugar on a daily basis, this Honey Nut Popcorn is still one of my favorite flavors.

1. Place popcorn in a large bowl. Remove any unpopped or partially popped kernels.

2. Place butter and peanut butter in a microwave safe bowl and cover with a paper towel. Microwave for 30 seconds at a time until melted. Add honey and mix well. Pour over popcorn and stir to coat. Add peanuts and stir again. Store in an airtight container for up to one week.

HOT CHOCOLATE

INGREDIENTS:

10–12 cups popped popcorn

¼ cup unsweetened cocoa powder

¼ cup granular coffee creamer

½ cup granulated sugar

½ cup unsalted butter

1 cup mini marshmallows

In a hurry? You can use 1 cup powdered hot cocoa mix in place of the unsweetened cocoa powder, coffee creamer, and sugar in this recipe. But don't skip the marshmallows!

1. Place popcorn in a large bowl. Remove any unpopped or partially popped kernels.

2. In a small bowl, mix together cocoa powder, coffee creamer, and sugar. Set aside.

3. Place butter in a microwave safe bowl and cover with a paper towel. Microwave for 30 seconds at a time until melted. Drizzle over popcorn and shake to coat. Sprinkle with the cocoa powder mixture and shake again. Add marshmallows and stir to combine. Store in an airtight container for up to one week.

Let me just give you a little bit of advice on this one. This popcorn is amazing. But don't be fooled into eating it all right away and then falling into a post-snack nap and forgetting about the dishes for days. That sugar in the pot is going to turn itself into a rock when it cools. Allow the pot to cool for a few minutes and then fill the bottom with water to make clean up easier.

INGREDIENTS:

¼ cup canola oil
½ cup popcorn kernels
⅓ cup sugar

1. Place a 3- to 4-quart pot on a stovetop and pour in oil. Be sure to use oil with a high smoke point such as peanut or canola oil. Drop 3 kernels into the pot. Place the lid on top. If the lid has a vent, open it to allow steam to escape. Heat the pot on medium-high heat. Listen for the kernels to pop.

2. When all 3 kernels have popped, quickly pour in popcorn kernels and sugar. Replace the lid and shake the pot back and forth to coat the kernels with oil. The pot will be very hot! Protect your hands.

3. Once the popping starts, gently shake the pot back and forth over the burner. When the popping slows, remove from heat and immediately pour into a serving bowl. Allow to cool. Store in an airtight container for up to one week.

KETTLE CORN

51

KEY LIME PIE

This recipe very nearly did me in. When my son learned I was going to make a popcorn book, Key Lime Pie Popcorn was his only flavor request. Of two things, he was absolutely certain: the popcorn should be green, and it should taste like lime pie. I tried countless variations before finding one that met with his stamp of approval.

INGREDIENTS:

10–12 cups popped popcorn
1 cup granulated sugar
½ cup water
1 Tbsp. unsalted butter
½ tsp. baking soda

1 packet unsweetened lime drink mix
1½ cups graham cereal
4 oz. white melting chocolate

• •

1. Place popcorn in a large bowl. Remove any unpopped or partially popped kernels.

2. In a medium saucepan, stir together sugar and water. Add butter and heat on medium high, stirring occasionally. When the mixture comes to a boil, allow to boil for 3 minutes without stirring. Remove from heat and immediately add baking soda and drink mix. Stir to combine. The mixture will be foamy. Pour over popcorn while still hot. Stir gently until the popcorn is completely coated.

3. Spread on parchment lined baking sheet to cool. Add graham cereal.

4. Place melting chocolate in a microwave safe bowl. Microwave for 30 seconds at a time, then stir. Repeat until completely melted. Drizzle over popcorn and allow to cool. Store in an airtight container for up to one week.

53

LEMON MERINGUE

My grandmother stayed with me for Thanksgiving one year. Her favorite pie ever is lemon meringue. I was determined to make it old school from scratch—just for her. I read all the recipes, and we made it together late at night. It didn't really seem right the next morning, so I asked her what I could have done wrong. And she told me, "I don't know. I always make it from a box." I've never made a lemon meringue pie since then. Luckily, with this recipe, you can skip the crust and the uncertainty of actual meringue and go straight to the tangy sweet goodness!

INGREDIENTS:

10–12 cups popped popcorn
1 cup granulated sugar
½ cup water
1 Tbsp. unsalted butter
½ tsp. baking soda

2 tsp. lemon flavoring
1–2 drops yellow food coloring (optional)
2 cups mini marshmallows

1. Place popcorn in a large bowl. Remove any unpopped or partially popped kernels.

2. In a medium saucepan, stir together sugar and water. Add butter and heat on medium high, stirring occasionally. When the mixture comes to a boil, allow to boil for 3 minutes without stirring. Remove from heat and immediately add baking soda, lemon flavoring, and food coloring if using. Stir to combine. The mixture will be foamy. Pour over popcorn while still hot. Stir gently until the popcorn is completely coated. Add marshmallows and stir again. Marshmallows will melt into the candy coating. Allow to cool. Store in an airtight container for up to one week.

LEMON POPPY SEED

INGREDIENTS:

10–12 cups popped popcorn
1 cup granulated sugar
¼ cup lemon juice
1 Tbsp. unsalted butter
½ tsp. baking soda

1 tsp. butter flavoring
1 tsp. almond flavoring
1 Tbsp. poppy seeds

There is just something about lemon and poppy seeds that makes my mouth happy. And this sweet, gooey, beautiful mess of a popcorn is no exception! You could also try adding a teaspoon of orange flavor to give it more of a citrus pop!

1. Place popcorn in a large bowl. Remove any unpopped or partially popped kernels.

2. In a medium saucepan, stir together sugar and lemon juice. Add butter and heat on medium high, stirring occasionally. When the mixture comes to a boil, allow to boil for 3 minutes without stirring. Remove from heat and immediately add baking soda and flavorings. Stir to combine. The mixture will be foamy. Pour over popcorn while still hot. Stir gently until the popcorn is completely coated. Sprinkle poppy seeds over popcorn and stir again. Allow to cool. Store in an airtight container for up to one week.

INGREDIENTS:

10–12 cups popped popcorn
½ cup unsalted butter
½ cup maple syrup
1 cup powdered sugar

Maple Bar Popcorn was a surprising favorite at my house! I'm not sure if purchasing a dozen maple bars for "inspiration" had anything to do with my children's love of this flavor, but this popcorn didn't last long around here!

1. Place popcorn in a large bowl. Remove any unpopped or partially popped kernels.

2. Place butter and syrup in a microwave safe bowl and cover with a paper towel. Microwave for 30 seconds at a time until melted. Whisk together. Pour over popcorn and stir to coat. Cover with powdered sugar and stir to evenly distribute. Store in an airtight container for up to one week.

MAPLE BAR

MINT COOKIE

INGREDIENTS:

10–12 cups popped popcorn

1½ cups broken chocolate graham crackers or chocolate animal crackers

1½ cups mint chocolate chips

Don't limit your love of cool-mint chocolate-covered grahams to a single season! This winning combination is hard to beat year-round!

1. Place popcorn in a large bowl. Remove any unpopped or partially popped kernels. Add broken crackers.

2. Place chocolate chips in a microwave safe bowl. Microwave for 30 seconds at a time, stirring in between, until completely melted. Pour over popcorn and broken crackers, and stir to coat. Allow to cool. Store in an airtight container for up to one week.

MINT PATTY

INGREDIENTS:

10–12 cups popped popcorn
¼ cup unsalted butter
2 Tbsp. light corn syrup
1 Tbsp. peppermint extract
1 cup powdered sugar
6 oz. melting chocolate

The cooling mint mixed with mellow chocolate is a winning flavor combination! If using peppermint oil instead of peppermint extract, 3–4 drops should be enough. Peppermint oil is VERY concentrated!

1. Place popcorn in a large bowl. Remove any unpopped or partially popped kernels.

2. Place butter and corn syrup in a microwave safe bowl and cover with a paper towel. Microwave for 30 seconds at a time until melted and smooth. Add peppermint extract and powdered sugar. Mix well. Pour over popcorn and stir to coat.

3. Place melting chocolate in a microwave safe bowl. Microwave for 30 seconds at a time, stirring in between, until completely melted. Pour over popcorn and stir just until evenly distributed. Allow to cool. Store in an airtight container for up to one week.

INGREDIENTS:

10–12 cups popped popcorn
¼ cup unsalted butter
¼ cup flour
¼ cup granulated sugar
1 cup old fashioned oats
1 cup granulated sugar

½ cup water
1 Tbsp. unsalted butter
½ tsp. baking soda
1 tsp. vanilla
1 tsp. cinnamon
1 cup raisins

1. Place popcorn in a large bowl. Remove any unpopped or partially popped kernels.

2. In a small bowl, mix ¼ cup butter, ¼ cup flour, and ¼ cup granulated sugar until completely combined. Stir in the oats and set bowl aside.

3. In a medium saucepan, stir together 1 cup sugar and ½ cup water. Add 1 tablespoon butter and heat on medium high, stirring occasionally. When the mixture comes to a boil, allow to boil for 3 minutes without stirring. Remove from heat and immediately add baking soda, vanilla, and cinnamon. Stir to combine. The mixture will be foamy. Pour over popcorn while still hot. Stir gently until the popcorn is completely coated. Add the oatmeal crumb mixture and raisins and stir again. Allow to cool before serving.

OATMEAL RAISIN

ORANGE CREAM

INGREDIENTS:

10–12 cups popped popcorn

1 cup granulated sugar

½ cup water

1 Tbsp. unsalted butter

½ tsp. baking soda

2 tsp. orange flavoring

1–2 drops orange food coloring (optional)

1 cup white chocolate chips

Is there any flavor dreamier than orange cream? If you want a more blended flavor, try substituting the white chocolate chips with 6 ounces of melted white melting chocolate. Pour over the popcorn after it has been coated with the orange flavoring.

1. Place popcorn in a large bowl. Remove any unpopped or partially popped kernels.

2. In a medium saucepan, stir together sugar and water. Add butter and heat on medium high, stirring occasionally. When the mixture comes to a boil, allow to boil for 3 minutes without stirring. Remove from heat and immediately add baking soda, flavoring, and food coloring if using. Stir to combine. The mixture will be foamy. Pour over popcorn while still hot. Stir gently until the popcorn is completely coated. Add white chocolate chips and stir again. Allow to cool. Store in an airtight container for up to one week.

PEACH COBBLER

INGREDIENTS:

10–12 cups popped popcorn

¼ cup unsalted butter

1 cup yellow cake mix

6 oz. white melting chocolate

1 cup chopped peach gummy candies

A fun twist on a traditional favorite flavor combination! Try rubbing cooking oil on your knife before cutting the candies to keep them from sticking.

1. Place popcorn in a large bowl. Remove any unpopped or partially popped kernels.

2. Mix butter and cake mix in a small bowl until it looks like coarse crumbs. Set aside.

3. Place melting chocolate in a microwave safe bowl. Microwave for 30 seconds at a time, stirring in between, until completely melted. Pour over popcorn and stir to coat. Sprinkle cake mix mixture over popcorn and stir to coat again. Add peach candies and stir to evenly distribute. Store in an airtight container for up to one week.

PEANUT BUTTER

Lightly sweet and perfectly salty, this is a peanut-lover's dream! Try substituting the peanut butter and peanuts with other nut butters such as almond butter or sunflower seed butter for fun new flavors!

INGREDIENTS:

10–12 cups popped popcorn
½ cup unsalted butter
½ cup peanut butter
½ cup powdered sugar
1 tsp. vanilla
¼ tsp. salt
½ cup peanuts

1. Place popcorn in a large bowl. Remove any unpopped or partially popped kernels.

2. Place butter and peanut butter in a microwave safe bowl and cover with a paper towel. Microwave for 30 seconds at a time until melted. Add powdered sugar, vanilla, and salt, and whisk together until completely combined. Pour over popcorn and stir to coat. Add peanuts. Store in an airtight container for up to one week.

PEANUT BUTTER AND JAM

When testing this recipe, it was clear that people have a favorite of the two flavors! Some people wanted more jam flavoring and an equal number of people wanted a stronger peanut butter flavor. If serving at a party, try leaving the two different flavors of popcorn separate and let people make their own mix!

INGREDIENTS:

5–6 cups popped popcorn
2/3 cup peanut butter chips
5–6 cups popcorn
4 oz. white melting chocolate
1/4 cup jam

1. Place popcorn in 2 separate bowls. Remove any unpopped or partially popped kernels.

2. For peanut butter popcorn: Place peanut butter chips in a microwave safe bowl. Microwave for 30 seconds at a time, stirring in between, until completely melted. Pour over popcorn and stir to coat. Allow to cool.

3. For jam popcorn: Place melting chocolate in a microwave safe bowl. Microwave for 30 seconds at a time, stirring in between, until completely melted. Add jam and stir again. Quickly pour over popcorn and stir to coat. Allow to cool.

4. When both popcorns are cool, combine in a large bowl. Store in an airtight container for up to one week.

PEANUT BUTTER COOKIES AND CREAM

INGREDIENTS:

10–12 cups popped popcorn

1½ cup peanut butter chips

1½ cup crumbled sandwich cookies (about 15 cookies)

I LOVE cookies-and-cream-flavored anything. (Maybe not Chap Stick. That would be weird. But certainly, any food.) I didn't think the original Cookies and Cream Popcorn could be improved upon, but this recipe might just be even better than the first! As always, be mindful of food allergies when serving nut recipes. People probably won't expect nuts to be mixed with Cookies and Cream!

1. Place popcorn in a large bowl. Remove any unpopped or partially popped kernels.

2. Place peanut butter chips in a microwave safe bowl. Microwave for 30 seconds at a time, stirring in between, until completely melted. Pour over popcorn and stir to coat. Add cookie pieces and stir again. Allow to cool. Store in an airtight container for up to one week.

INGREDIENTS:

10–12 cups popped popcorn
½ cup unsalted butter
½ cup creamy peanut butter
½ cup brown sugar
¼ tsp. salt
4 oz. melting chocolate

The only thing that could possibly make this popcorn better would be adding mini or broken-up peanut butter cups to the popcorn after it has cooled! You should definitely do that.

1. Place popcorn in a large bowl. Remove any unpopped or partially popped kernels.

2. Place butter and peanut butter in a microwave safe bowl and cover with a paper towel. Microwave for 30 seconds at a time until melted. Add brown sugar and salt and mix until combined. Pour over popcorn and stir to coat. Spread on parchment lined baking sheet.

3. Place melting chocolate in a microwave safe bowl. Microwave for 30 seconds at a time, stirring in between, until completely melted. Drizzle over popcorn and allow to cool. Store in an airtight container for up to one week.

PEANUT BUTTER CUP

PIÑA COLADA

INGREDIENTS:

10–12 cups popped popcorn
6 oz. white melting chocolate
1 cup dried pineapple, chopped
½ cup shredded coconut

The light, refreshing flavor of pineapple and coconut combined is perfect for warm summer months AND cold winter months when you WANT it to be warm summer months! Feel free to change the ratio of coconut and pineapple to suit your preferences!

1. Place popcorn in a large bowl. Remove any unpopped or partially popped kernels.

2. Place melting chocolate in a microwave safe bowl. Microwave for 30 seconds, then stir. Repeat until completely melted. Pour over popcorn and stir to coat. Add pineapple and coconut and stir again. Allow to cool. Store in an airtight container for up to one week.

POMEGRANATE

INGREDIENTS:

10–12 cups popped popcorn
1 cup sugar
1 cup pomegranate juice
1 Tbsp. unsalted butter
½ tsp. baking soda

They key to this unique popcorn flavor is definitely patience! The juice has to boil for a full 12 minutes so that it can cook down into a syrup! Don't skimp on the cook time, or the popcorn will be a sticky mess.

1. Place popcorn in a large bowl. Remove any unpopped or partially popped kernels.

2. In a medium saucepan, stir together sugar and pomegranate juice. Add butter and heat on medium high, stirring occasionally. When the mixture comes to a boil, allow to boil for 12 minutes without stirring. Remove from heat and immediately add baking soda. Stir to combine. The mixture will be foamy. Pour over popcorn while still hot. Stir gently until the popcorn is completely coated. Allow to cool. Store in an airtight container for up to one week.

INGREDIENTS:

10–12 cups popped popcorn
½ cup unsalted butter
½ cup brown sugar
¼ cup granulated sugar
1 tsp. cinnamon
½ tsp. ginger
½ tsp. nutmeg
¼ tsp. allspice

If you don't have (or want) a spice cabinet the size of a coat closet, you can still make this Pumpkin Spice Popcorn! Just use 2 teaspoons pumpkin spice in place of the cinnamon, ginger, nutmeg, and allspice!

1. Place popcorn in a large bowl. Remove any unpopped or partially popped kernels.

2. Place butter in a microwave safe bowl and cover with a paper towel. Microwave for 30 seconds at a time until melted. Add brown sugar, sugar, cinnamon, ginger, nutmeg, and allspice. Mix well. Pour over popcorn and stir to coat. Store in an airtight container for up to one week.

PUMPKIN SPICE

RED VELVET

INGREDIENTS:
10–12 cups popped popcorn
6 oz. white melting chocolate
1 cup red velvet cake mix

The red food coloring can (and will!) color fingers and mouths. I don't want to boss your popcorn, but it's probably best not to serve this at a formal event.

1. Place popcorn in a large bowl. Remove any unpopped or partially popped kernels.

2. Place melting chocolate in a microwave safe bowl. Microwave for 30 seconds at a time, stirring in between, until completely melted. Pour over popcorn and stir to coat. Sprinkle cake mix over popcorn and stir gently to evenly distribute. Allow to cool. Store in an airtight container for up to one week.

ROCKY ROAD

I didn't know this before making this recipe, but apparently there is a little drama in the Rocky Road flavor world. People are either Team Almonds or Team Peanuts. I chose to use almonds, but you can just as easily switch those out for peanuts if you prefer!

INGREDIENTS:

10–12 cups popped popcorn

6 oz. melting chocolate

1 cup mini marshmallows

½ cup chopped roasted almonds

1. Place popcorn in a large bowl. Remove any un-popped or partially popped kernels.

2. Place melting chocolate in a microwave safe bowl. Microwave for 30 seconds at a time, stirring in between, until completely melted. Pour over popcorn and stir to coat. Add marshmallows and almonds and stir again. Allow to cool. Store in an airtight container for up to one week.

ROOT BEER FLOAT

INGREDIENTS:

10–12 cups popped popcorn

1 cup granulated sugar

½ cup water

1 Tbsp. unsalted butter

½ tsp. baking soda

1 Tbsp. root beer flavoring

4 oz. white melting chocolate

There are many different brands of root beer extract. Some of them have a darker color than others. So, don't be alarmed if your root beer popcorn is a paler shade than mine! You can always add a few drops of brown food coloring if you want more color.

1. Place popcorn in a large bowl. Remove any unpopped or partially popped kernels.

2. In a medium saucepan, stir together sugar and water. Add butter and heat on medium high, stirring occasionally. When the mixture comes to a boil, allow to boil for 3 minutes without stirring. Remove from heat and immediately add baking soda and root beer flavoring. Stir to combine. The mixture will be foamy. Pour over popcorn while still hot. Stir gently until the popcorn is completely coated. Spread on parchment lined baking sheet to cool.

3. Place melting chocolate in a microwave safe bowl. Microwave for 30 seconds, then stir. Repeat until completely melted. Drizzle over popcorn. Allow to cool. Store in an airtight container for up to one week.

INGREDIENTS:

10–12 cups popped popcorn
2 Tbsp. unsalted butter
4 cups mini marshmallows
2/3 cup chocolate chips
1 cup graham cereal

Satisfy your s'mores craving in just minutes! No fire and no lingering smoke smell required!

1. Place popcorn in a large bowl. Remove any unpopped or partially popped kernels.

2. Place butter and marshmallows in a microwave safe bowl. Microwave for 60 seconds and stir. Repeat at 30 second intervals until marshmallows are completely melted. Pour over popcorn and stir to coat. Allow to cool slightly (1–2 minutes) and then add chocolate chips and cereal. Store in an airtight container for up to one week.

S'MORES

INGREDIENTS:

10–12 cups popped popcorn
6 oz. white melting chocolate
1 packet unsweetened cherry drink mix powder

Because the drink powder is not mixed with water, it won't color the popcorn. If you want your popcorn extra sour, add a second drink mix packet!

1. Place popcorn in a large bowl. Remove any unpopped or partially popped kernels.

2. Place melting chocolate in a microwave safe bowl. Microwave for 30 seconds at a time, stirring in between, until completely melted. Add drink mix powder and stir quickly. Immediately pour over popcorn and stir to coat. Store in an airtight container for up to one week.

SOUR CHERRY

SPICED CARAMEL APPLE

INGREDIENTS:

10–12 cups popped popcorn

6 oz. white melting chocolate

¼ cup apple cider drink mix (about 2 packets)

1½ cup caramel bits (about 11 oz)

4 tsp. water

To say this was popular with the neighborhood children would be an understatement. The light tartness of the apple drink mix brings a perfect balance to the sweet caramel. Apple cider drink mix can generally be found near the hot cocoa powders.

1. Place popcorn in a large bowl. Remove any unpopped or partially popped kernels.

2. Place melting chocolate in a microwave safe bowl. Microwave for 30 seconds at a time, stirring in between, until completely melted. Pour over popcorn and stir to coat. Sprinkle with apple drink mix and stir again to coat. Spread on parchment lined baking sheet to cool.

3. Place caramel bits and water in a microwave safe bowl. Microwave for 30 seconds and stir. Repeat until completely melted and smooth. Drizzle over popcorn. Allow to cool. Store in an airtight container for up to one week.

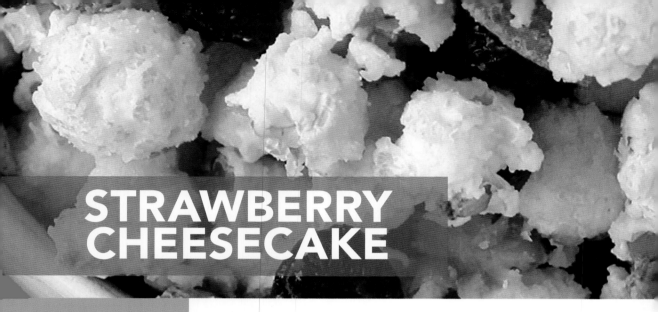

STRAWBERRY CHEESECAKE

The white chocolate is poured over the popcorn before the cream cheese mixture so that it can act as a barrier to the moisture in the cream cheese mixture. If you accidentally pour the cream cheese mixture over the popcorn first, you might end up with soggy popcorn.

INGREDIENTS:

10–12 cups popped popcorn
6 oz. white melting chocolate
4 oz. cream cheese
1 Tbsp. butter

1 cup graham cereal
½ cup strawberry flavored cranberry raisins

1. Place popcorn in a large bowl. Remove any unpopped or partially popped kernels.

2. Place melting chocolate in a microwave safe bowl. Microwave for 30 seconds at a time, stirring in between, until completely melted. Place cream cheese and butter in another microwave safe bowl and melt for 30 seconds and stir. Repeat until completely melted. Pour melted white chocolate over the popcorn and stir to coat. Immediately add the melted cream cheese mixture and stir again. Pour graham cereal and strawberry flavored cranberry raisins over the popcorn. Serve immediately.

SUGAR COOKIE

While pink is probably the most recognized sugar cookie frosting color, you could definitely make the frosting glaze in this recipe any color you choose! I'd recommend staying away from swamp green . . . but I'm not going to judge you if that's your thing.

INGREDIENTS:

10–12 cups popped popcorn
1/2 cup unsalted butter
1/4 cup flour
1 tsp. vanilla
1/8 tsp. salt

1/4 cup unsalted butter
1 tsp. vanilla
1–2 drops pink food coloring
1/2 cup powdered sugar
2 Tbsp. sprinkles

1. Place popcorn in a large bowl. Remove any unpopped or partially popped kernels.

2. Place 1/2 cup butter in a microwave safe bowl and cover with a paper towel. Microwave for 30 seconds at a time until melted. Add flour, 1 tsp. vanilla, and salt. Mix well. Pour over popcorn and stir to coat. Spread on parchment lined baking sheet to cool.

3. Place 1/4 cup butter in a microwave safe bowl and cover with a paper towel. Microwave for 30 seconds at a time until melted. Add 1 tsp. vanilla, food coloring, and powdered sugar. Mix well. Drizzle over popcorn. Add sprinkles. Store in an airtight container for up to one week.

INGREDIENTS:

10–12 cups popped popcorn
¾ cup unsalted butter
¾ cup granulated sugar
1 tsp. vanilla
4 oz. melting chocolate

1. Place popcorn in a large bowl. Remove any unpopped or partially popped kernels.

2. In a medium saucepan, heat butter and sugar on medium high. Stir constantly until it turns a golden amber color. Remove from heat and add vanilla. Mix quickly and pour over popcorn. Stir quickly to coat. Spread on parchment lined baking sheet. Break apart when cool.

3. Place melting chocolate in a microwave safe bowl. Microwave for 30 seconds at a time, stirring in between, until completely melted. Drizzle over popcorn. Allow to cool. Store in an airtight container for up to one week.

TOFFEE

TRAIL MIX

INGREDIENTS:

10–12 cups popped popcorn

4 oz. white melting chocolate

4 cups total of the following: chocolate candies, raisins, yogurt-covered raisins, dried cranberries, peanuts, and marshmallows

The possibilities here are endless! You could add a little of everything or a lot of just one thing. (My children would recommend that one thing to be chocolate candies.) You could also try adding whole grain cereals, crackers, or even pretzel bites!

1. Place popcorn in a large bowl. Remove any unpopped or partially popped kernels.

2. Place melting chocolate in a microwave safe bowl. Microwave for 30 seconds at a time, stirring in between, until completely melted. Pour over popcorn and stir to coat. Add candy-raisin mix and stir again. Store in an airtight container for up to one week.

TROPICAL

INGREDIENTS:

10–12 cups popped popcorn

1 cup granulated sugar

1/2 cup water

1 Tbsp. unsalted butter

1/2 tsp. baking soda

2 tsp. coconut flavoring

1/3 cup banana chips

1/3 cup dried mango, chopped

1/3 cup shredded coconut

1/3 cup dried pineapple, chopped

The sweet coconut candy coating is the perfect bridge between all of the added fruits in this Tropical Popcorn! Wipe a little cooking oil on your knife before chopping the fruits to keep them from sticking to the knife.

1. Place popcorn in a large bowl. Remove any unpopped or partially popped kernels.

2. In a medium saucepan, stir together sugar and water. Add butter and heat on medium high, stirring occasionally. When the mixture comes to a boil, allow to boil for 3 minutes without stirring. Remove from heat and immediately add baking soda and coconut flavoring. Stir to combine. The mixture will be foamy. Pour over popcorn while still hot. Stir gently until the popcorn is completely coated. Add banana chips, mango, coconut, and pineapple, and stir again. Allow to cool. Store in an airtight container for up to one week.

INGREDIENTS:

10–12 cups popped popcorn
2 cups horn shaped corn snacks
6 oz. white melting chocolate
1 cup colorful cereal flakes
2 tsp. nonpareils

Both the boys and girls in my neighborhood were delighted with the "horns" in this Unicorn Popcorn recipe. If you live near a craft store, you can add a little more magic with some edible glitter sugar from the cake decorating aisle. Horn shaped corn snacks can generally be found in the chip aisle of most grocery stores.

1. Place popcorn on a parchment lined baking sheet. Remove any unpopped or partially popped kernels. Add corn snacks.

2. Place melting chocolate in a microwave safe bowl. Microwave for 30 seconds at a time, stirring in between, until completely melted. Drizzle over popcorn. Sprinkle with cereal flakes and nonpareils. Stir gently and allow to cool. Store in an airtight container for up to one week.

UNICORN

WHITE CHOCOLATE CHIP MOLASSES

INGREDIENTS:

10–12 cups popped popcorn

1/2 cup unsalted butter

1/3 cup molasses

1/3 cup brown sugar

1/2 tsp. cinnamon

1/4 tsp. nutmeg

1 cup white chocolate chips

People either love or hate molasses. I think it's because molasses can be a little bossy. It tends to overwhelm the flavors around it. White chocolate seems to be that perfect friend that helps mellow the flavor without changing it.

1. Place popcorn in a large bowl. Remove any unpopped or partially popped kernels.

2. Place butter and molasses in a microwave safe bowl and cover with a paper towel. Microwave for 30 seconds at a time until melted. Add brown sugar, cinnamon, and nutmeg. Mix well. Pour over popcorn and stir to coat. Add white chocolate chips and stir again. Store in an airtight container for up to one week.

89

WHITE CHOCOLATE MACADAMIA NUT

INGREDIENTS:
10–12 cups popped popcorn
6 oz. white melting chocolate
1 cup chopped macadamia nuts

This is my favorite kind of recipe—simple and delicious! There are an increasing number of roasted macadamia nut flavors available at the grocery store: natural, salted, unsalted, honey roasted, etc. Try them all to find your favorite! (My favorite with this recipe is honey roasted because I LOVE sugar.)

1. Place popcorn in a large bowl. Remove any unpopped or partially popped kernels.

2. Place melting chocolate in a microwave safe bowl. Microwave for 30 seconds at a time, stirring in between, until completely melted. Pour over popcorn and stir to coat. Add macadamia nuts and stir again. Allow to cool. Store in an airtight container for up to one week.

INGREDIENTS:

10–12 cups popped popcorn
4 oz. melting chocolate
4 oz. white melting chocolate

1. Place popcorn on a parchment lined baking sheet. Remove any unpopped or partially popped kernels.

2. Place melting chocolates in separate microwave safe bowls. Microwave separately for 30 seconds at a time, stirring in between, until completely melted. Alternating white and chocolate, drizzle over popcorn in opposite directions. Allow to cool. Store in an airtight container for up to one week.

ZEBRA

SAVORY

BAKED POTATO

In the perfect mix between potato chips and popcorn, this Baked Potato Popcorn really does taste like roasted potato with everything on it! Cheese powder can generally be found in the popcorn aisle or near the spices in the baking aisle of a grocery store.

INGREDIENTS:

10–12 cups popped popcorn
½ cup potato flakes
¼ cup buttermilk powder
2 Tbsp. cheese powder
2 Tbsp. bacon bits

½ tsp. salt
Butter flavor oil spray
2 Tbsp. chopped fresh chives

1. Place popcorn in a large bowl. Remove any unpopped or partially popped kernels.

2. Combine potato flakes, buttermilk powder, cheese powder, bacon bits, and salt in a food processor. Pulse until powdery.

3. Spray the top layer of the popcorn with the oil spray and then sprinkle with about 2 tablespoons of the potato flake mixture. Stir gently to bring plain popcorn to the surface. Continue spraying with oil and sprinkling with the potato flake mixture until fully coated. Store in an airtight container for up to one week. Sprinkle with fresh chives before serving.

BARBECUE

INGREDIENTS:

10–12 cups popped popcorn
1/3 cup brown sugar
1/3 cup molasses
1/2 cup ketchup
1 tsp. onion powder
1 tsp. ground mustard

1/2 tsp. garlic powder
1 tsp. paprika
1/4 tsp. ground black pepper
1/4 tsp. salt
1/2 tsp. baking soda
1 Tbsp. vinegar

This full-flavored Barbecue Popcorn would make the PERFECT tailgating or game day snack! And the best part is that you can make it ahead of time so you can focus all your attention on your favorite team!

1. Place popcorn in a large bowl. Remove any unpopped or partially popped kernels.

2. In a medium saucepan, stir together brown sugar, molasses, and ketchup. Heat on medium high, stirring occasionally. When the mixture comes to a boil, allow to boil for 5 minutes without stirring. Meanwhile, mix together onion powder, mustard, garlic powder, paprika, pepper, salt, and baking soda in a small bowl. Remove molasses mixture from heat and immediately add the spice mixture. Stir quickly and then add the vinegar. Stir again. Pour over popcorn and gently stir to coat. Spread on a parchment lined baking sheet to cool. Store in an airtight container for up to one week.

BROWN BUTTER

INGREDIENTS:

½ cup salted butter
¼ cup popcorn kernels

I'm not going to lie. I just really wanted to see what would happen if you tried to make microwave popcorn with butter already in the bowl. MAGIC HAPPENS. That's what. Sometimes there is still just a little bit of butter in the bottom of the bowl after the popcorn is done popping. I like to transfer the popcorn to another bowl and then pour that little bit of leftover brown butter on top. If you like brown butter, you HAVE to try this recipe!

1. Place butter and popcorn kernels in the bottom of a glass bowl that will hold at least 8 cups. Cover with a microwave safe plate. Try to choose a plate that doesn't completely seal off the top of the bowl, so that steam can escape. Microwave for 6–9 minutes. The butter will melt and begin to boil. The popcorn will start to pop as the butter gets foamy. Remove from the microwave when the popping slows. Be very careful! The bowl will be HOT. Allow to cool. Store in an airtight container for up to one week.

BUFFALO WING

INGREDIENTS:

10–12 cups popped popcorn

3 Tbsp. unsalted butter

2 Tbsp. hot pepper sauce

1/8 tsp. garlic powder

1/8 tsp. onion powder

1/8 tsp. salt

If you love spicy flavors, you may be tempted to add more hot sauce to this popcorn. Unfortunately, it will just make the popcorn soggy. Try adding some cayenne pepper instead!

1. Place popcorn in a large bowl. Remove any unpopped or partially popped kernels.

2. Place butter in a microwave safe bowl and cover with a paper towel. Microwave for 30 seconds at a time until melted. Add hot sauce, garlic powder, onion powder, and salt. Mix well. Drizzle half of the mixture over popcorn and shake to coat. Repeat with remaining mixture. Serve immediately.

INGREDIENTS:
10–12 cups popped popcorn
½ cup unsalted butter
½ tsp. salt

It's hard to improve on a timeless classic like buttered popcorn...but for extra butter flavoring, sprinkle with butter powder from the popcorn or baking aisle!

1. Place popcorn in a large bowl. Remove any unpopped or partially popped kernels.

2. Place butter in a microwave safe bowl and cover with a paper towel. Microwave for 30 seconds at a time until melted. Add salt and mix well. Drizzle over popcorn and shake to coat. Serve immediately.

BUTTER

INGREDIENTS:

10–12 cups popped popcorn
1/2 cup unsalted butter
2 tsp. paprika
3/4 tsp. salt
1/2 tsp. garlic powder

1/2 tsp. onion powder
1/2 tsp. dried thyme
1/2 tsp. dried oregano
1/8 tsp. black pepper
1/8 tsp. cayenne pepper

1. Place popcorn in a large bowl. Remove any unpopped or partially popped kernels.

2. Place butter in a microwave safe bowl and cover with a paper towel. Microwave for 30 seconds at a time until melted. Add spices and mix well. Drizzle over popcorn and shake to coat. Serve immediately.

CAJUN

INGREDIENTS:

10–12 cups popped popcorn
1 cup shredded cheddar cheese
½ cup chopped cooked bacon
Salt and pepper

If you want extra bacon flavor, cook the bacon before making your popcorn. Pop your popcorn using the stovetop method from the beginning of the book and use the bacon grease in place of the oil!

1. Place popcorn on a parchment lined baking sheet. Remove any unpopped or partially popped kernels.

2. Sprinkle with shredded cheese and bacon. Add salt and pepper to taste. Broil for 1–2 minutes, or until cheese is melted. Serve immediately.

CHEDDAR BACON

CHEESEBURGER

INGREDIENTS:
10–12 cups popped popcorn
1/3 cup cheese powder
4 tsp. powdered beef bouillon
Butter flavor oil spray

For the carnivore in your life that just can't get enough meat, there's Cheeseburger Popcorn! Cheese powder can generally be found in the popcorn aisle or near the spices in the baking aisle of a grocery store.

1. Place popcorn in a large bowl. Remove any unpopped or partially popped kernels.

2. In a small bowl, mix cheese powder and beef bouillon. Spray the top layer of the popcorn with the oil spray and then sprinkle with about 2 tablespoons of the cheese mixture. Stir gently to bring plain popcorn to the surface. Continue spraying with oil and sprinkling with the cheese mixture until fully coated. Store in an airtight container for up to one week.

CHIPOTLE

INGREDIENTS:

10–12 cups popped popcorn

1/2 cup unsalted butter

1/2 tsp. chipotle chili pepper powder

1/4 tsp. salt

1/4 tsp. paprika

1/4 tsp. onion powder

1/4 tsp. garlic powder

1/8 tsp. ground black pepper

1 cup plain corn nuts

If you like your popcorn bold and smoky, I've got you covered with this not-too-spicy Chipotle Popcorn. If you can't find corn nuts, small corn chips are a great substitute!

1. Place popcorn in a large bowl. Remove any unpopped or partially popped kernels.

2. Place butter in a microwave safe bowl and cover with a paper towel. Microwave for 30 seconds at a time until melted. Add spices to melted butter and mix well. Drizzle over popcorn and shake to coat. Add corn nuts. Serve immediately.

INGREDIENTS:

10–12 cups popped popcorn
½ cup unsalted butter
1 Tbsp. yellow curry powder
1 tsp. coconut flavoring
2 Tbsp. granulated sugar
1 cup pistachios
1 cup golden raisins
1 cup broken pita chip pieces

This crisp, yellow, buttery curry goodness in popcorn form was a little bit of a surprise for me. It tastes exactly the way curry should taste, but what I didn't expect was how PERFECTLY curry and popcorn go together! Try using the stovetop popping method and use coconut oil for an extra boost of flavor.

1. Place popcorn in a large bowl. Remove any unpopped or partially popped kernels.

2. Place butter in a microwave safe bowl and cover with a paper towel. Microwave for 30 seconds at a time until melted. Add curry powder, coconut flavoring, and sugar. Mix well. Drizzle over popcorn and shake to coat. Add pistachios, raisins, and pita chips, and stir to combine. Store in an airtight container for up to one week.

CURRY

Shaking the popcorn instead of stirring to coat the popcorn with flavoring helps keep the popcorn crisp instead of soggy. Add freshly chopped hot peppers if you need more heat!

INGREDIENTS:

10–12 cups popped popcorn
¼ cup unsalted butter
1 Tbsp. red pepper sauce
1 tsp. cayenne pepper
1 tsp. crushed red pepper flakes

1 tsp. paprika
¼ tsp. garlic
½ tsp. onion powder
¼ tsp. salt

1. Place popcorn in a large bowl. Remove any unpopped or partially popped kernels.

2. Place butter in a microwave safe bowl and cover with a paper towel. Microwave for 30 seconds at a time until melted. Add red pepper sauce and spices. Mix well. Drizzle over popcorn and shake to coat. Serve immediately.

FIRE

FRENCH ONION

INGREDIENTS:
10–12 cups popped popcorn
½ cup unsalted butter
1 package french onion soup mix
2 cups crispy fried onions

I'm going to let you in on a little secret. Those crispy fried onions are sold in the CANNED VEGETABLE aisle at the grocery store. I've only ever purchased them around the holidays when they are displayed everywhere! As it turns out, they are NOT sold on endcaps during the summer. I spent weeks looking for them. Don't be like me. Look for them in the canned vegetable aisle near the green beans.

1. Place popcorn in a large bowl. Remove any unpopped or partially popped kernels.

2. Place butter in a microwave safe bowl and cover with a paper towel. Microwave for 30 seconds at a time until melted. Add soup mix and whisk until smooth. Pour over popcorn and stir to coat. Add fried onions and serve immediately.

INGREDIENTS:

10–12 cups popped popcorn

½ cup unsalted butter

½ tsp. garlic powder

½ tsp. onion powder

1 tsp. dried basil

¼ tsp. salt

½ cup parmesan cheese

This Garlic Herb Popcorn has all the comforting flavors of fresh baked garlic bread without having to wait! You can substitute the dried basil with 1 tablespoon chopped fresh basil if you enjoy fresh herbs.

1. Place popcorn in a large bowl. Remove any unpopped or partially popped kernels.

2. Place butter in a microwave safe bowl and cover with a paper towel. Microwave for 30 seconds at a time until melted. Add garlic powder, onion powder, basil, and salt to the butter and stir well. Drizzle over popcorn and stir quickly to coat. Sprinkle parmesan over popcorn and serve immediately.

GARLIC HERB

HONEY MUSTARD

INGREDIENTS:

10–12 cups popped popcorn

1/3 cup honey

1/3 cup brown sugar

2 Tbsp. water

1 Tbsp. unsalted butter

1/2 tsp. onion powder

1/2 tsp. salt

1/3 cup yellow mustard

1/4 tsp. baking soda

2 cups bite-size pretzels

There is never a wrong time to choose Honey Mustard Pretzel Popcorn! Feel free to use honey mustard instead of yellow mustard if you like a little more honey and a little less mustard!

1. Place popcorn in a large bowl. Remove any unpopped or partially popped kernels.

2. In a medium saucepan, stir together honey, brown sugar, and water. Add butter and heat on medium high, stirring occasionally. When the mixture comes to a boil, allow to boil for 5 minutes without stirring. Remove from heat and immediately add onion powder, salt, mustard, and baking soda. Stir to combine. Pour over popcorn while still hot. Stir gently until the popcorn is completely coated. Add pretzels and stir again. Store in an airtight container for up to one week.

JALAPEÑO POPPER

INGREDIENTS:

10–12 cups popped popcorn

3 Tbsp. unsalted butter

4 oz. cream cheese

1/4 tsp. salt

1/8 tsp. ground black pepper

1/2 cup chopped jalapeño peppers

Just like the real thing, this Jalapeño Popper Popcorn is best served hot and gooey! Make sure you chop the peppers before making the popcorn so they will be ready to add at the last minute.

1. Place popcorn in a large bowl. Remove any unpopped or partially popped kernels.

2. Place butter and cream cheese in a microwave safe bowl and cover with a paper towel. Microwave for 30 seconds at a time until melted. Add salt and black pepper. Mix well. Pour over popcorn and stir quickly to coat. Add chopped peppers and stir again. Serve immediately.

LEMON PEPPER

I love this recipe just the way it's written. But I also may have "accidentally" sprinkled it with some fresh grated parmesan cheese one day and it was AMAZING! Try it both ways and decide for yourself which one is your favorite!

INGREDIENTS:

10–12 cups popped popcorn
¼ cup unsalted butter
1 Tbsp. lemon juice
2 tsp. lemon zest
¼ tsp. ground black pepper
½ tsp. salt

....

1. Place popcorn in a large bowl. Remove any unpopped or partially popped kernels.

2. Place butter in a microwave safe bowl and cover with a paper towel. Microwave for 30 seconds at a time until melted. Add lemon juice, zest, pepper, and salt. Mix well. Drizzle over popcorn and shake to coat. Serve immediately.

INGREDIENTS:

10–12 cups popped popcorn

1/2 cup unsalted butter

1 cube tomato bouillon

1/4 cup buttermilk powder

1/4 cup granular coffee creamer

1/4 tsp. turmeric

1/4 tsp. cumin

1/4 tsp. coriander

1/8 tsp. cayenne

1/8 tsp. cinnamon

1/8 tsp. nutmeg

Did you know that traditional masala can contain up to 18 different ingredients? This not-too-spicy variation has just enough spices to give it the full body flavor without breaking the bank at the spice store.

1. Place popcorn in a large bowl. Remove any unpopped or partially popped kernels.

2. Place butter and bouillon cube in a microwave safe bowl and cover with a paper towel. Microwave for 30 seconds at a time until melted. Add remaining ingredients and mix well. Drizzle over popcorn and shake to coat. Serve immediately.

MASALA

NACHO

INGREDIENTS:
10–12 cups popped popcorn
¼ cup cheese powder
1 tsp. taco seasoning
Butter flavor oil spray

This Nacho Popcorn has just enough taco seasoning to make it solidly nacho flavored without overpowering the cheese flavor. Even my pickiest of eaters liked it! Feel free to add more taco seasoning if you love things a little spicier! Cheese powder can generally be found in the popcorn aisle or near the spices in the baking aisle of a grocery store.

1. Place popcorn in a large bowl. Remove any unpopped or partially popped kernels.

2. In a small bowl, mix cheese powder and taco seasoning. Spray the top layer of the popcorn with the oil spray and then sprinkle with about 2 tablespoons of the cheese mixture. Stir gently to bring plain popcorn to the surface. Continue spraying with oil and sprinkling with the cheese mixture until fully coated. Store in an airtight container for up to one week.

PAD THAI

INGREDIENTS:

10–12 cups popped popcorn

2 Tbsp. unsalted butter

2 Tbsp. creamy peanut butter

2 Tbsp. sesame oil

2 tsp. soy sauce

1 Tbsp. brown sugar

1 tsp. ketchup

1/2 tsp. salt

1/2 tsp. garlic

1/4 tsp. onion powder

1/8 tsp. cayenne

2 Tbsp. chopped fresh green onions

2 Tbsp. chopped peanuts

Enjoy all the flavors of one of the world's most popular Thai dishes—no fork necessary! Add a little more cayenne if you like your Thai on the spicy side!

1. Place popcorn in a large bowl. Remove any unpopped or partially popped kernels.

2. Place butter, peanut butter, and sesame oil in a microwave safe bowl and cover with a paper towel. Microwave for 30 seconds at a time until melted. Add soy sauce, brown sugar, ketchup, and spices and mix well. Pour over popcorn and stir to coat. Sprinkle with green onions and peanuts. Serve immediately.

INGREDIENTS:

10–12 cups popped popcorn
2 cups pretzel pieces
1/4 cup unsalted butter
2/3 cup creamy peanut butter
1/2 tsp. salt

Peanut butter pretzels, the well-loved snack that can't decide if it's sweet or savory, joins forces with another great snack of all time—popcorn—in this recipe that is perfect for after-school snacking, movies, and game night!

1. Place popcorn in a large bowl. Remove any unpopped or partially popped kernels. Add pretzel pieces and stir to evenly distribute.

2. Place butter and peanut butter in a microwave safe bowl and cover with a paper towel. Microwave for 30 seconds at a time until melted. Add salt and mix well. Pour over popcorn and stir to coat. Store in an airtight container for up to one week.

PEANUT BUTTER PRETZEL

PEPPERONI PIZZA

Try melting the cheese! After adding the cheese and pepperoni, place the popcorn in the microwave or an oven until the cheese is just melted. It tastes so much like real pizza, you could serve it for dinner!

INGREDIENTS:

10–12 cups popped popcorn
1/2 cup unsalted butter
1 tsp. dried oregano
1/2 tsp. onion powder
1/2 tsp. paprika
1/2 tsp. salt
1/8 tsp. garlic powder
1/8 tsp. ground black pepper
1 cup mini pepperoni
1 cup shredded cheese

1. Place popcorn in a large bowl. Remove any unpopped or partially popped kernels.

2. Place butter in a microwave safe bowl and cover with a paper towel. Microwave for 30 seconds at a time until melted. Add spices and mix well. Drizzle over popcorn and stir to coat. Sprinkle pepperoni and shredded cheese over popcorn and serve immediately.

PESTO

Traditional pesto is generally made with pine nuts. Walnuts are a low-cost and easy-to-find alternative that tastes almost the same as the original! If you have a discerning palate, or suddenly feel the need to try a blind taste test to determine if I'm right, you can substitute 2 tablespoons of finely chopped pine nuts in place of the walnuts.

INGREDIENTS:

10–12 cups popped popcorn

1/4 cup olive oil

1/4 cup finely chopped fresh basil leaves

2 Tbsp. finely chopped walnuts

1/4 tsp. garlic powder

1/4 tsp. salt

1/3 cup parmesan cheese

1. Place popcorn in a large bowl. Remove any unpopped or partially popped kernels.

2. In a small bowl, mix oil, basil, walnuts, garlic powder, and salt. Pour over popcorn and shake to coat. Sprinkle parmesan cheese over the top and stir to evenly distribute. Serve immediately.

121

INGREDIENTS:

10–12 cups popped popcorn
¼ tsp. garlic powder
½ tsp. onion powder
½ tsp. salt
¼ tsp. dried dill

1 tsp. dried parsley
1 Tbsp. buttermilk powder
½ cup unsalted butter
2 cups ranch flavored tortilla chips, broken in large pieces

In a hurry? You can substitute 4 teaspoons of ranch dressing seasoning mix for the spices and buttermilk in this recipe!

1. Place popcorn in a large bowl. Remove any unpopped or partially popped kernels.

2. In a small bowl, mix together garlic powder, onion powder, salt, dill, parsley, and buttermilk powder. Set aside.

3. Place butter in a microwave safe bowl and cover with a paper towel. Microwave for 30 seconds at a time until melted. Drizzle over popcorn and toss to coat. Sprinkle dry spice mix over popcorn and toss again. Add tortilla chips immediately before serving.

RANCH

ROSEMARY

INGREDIENTS:

10–12 cups popped popcorn

3 Tbsp. olive oil

1 Tbsp. chopped, fresh rosemary
(or 1 tsp. dried)

1/2 tsp. salt

1/4 tsp. garlic powder

Pinch of black pepper

1/3 cup grated parmesan cheese

If you've never used fresh rosemary before, it can be a little confusing to figure out how exactly you go about chopping it. Hold on to a sprig with one hand, and with the other hand, pull the leaves or needles down and against the growth to remove them from the stem. Discard the stem. Pile the needles together and chop across until they are as fine as you would like.

1. Place popcorn in a large bowl. Remove any unpopped or partially popped kernels.

2. In a small bowl, combine oil, rosemary, salt, garlic powder, and black pepper. Drizzle over popcorn and shake to coat. Sprinkle with parmesan cheese and stir again to distribute evenly. Serve immediately.

SALT AND VINEGAR

INGREDIENTS:

10–12 cups popped popcorn
¼ cup unsalted butter
1 Tbsp. white vinegar
½ tsp. cream of tartar
1 tsp. large grain salt

I'm a vinegar minimalist and use white or cider vinegar for most occasions that require vinegar. If you are an enthusiast, feel free to try a balsamic or wine vinegar in this recipe as well!

1. Place popcorn in a large bowl. Remove any unpopped or partially popped kernels.

2. Place butter in a microwave safe bowl and cover with a paper towel. Microwave for 30 seconds at a time until melted. Add vinegar and cream of tartar and mix well. Drizzle over popcorn and shake to coat. Sprinkle salt over popcorn. Serve immediately.

SAVORY SNACK MIX

There really is no wrong way to create this mix! Try adding other savory bite-size snacks in place of (or in addition to!) the pretzel pieces and peanuts. Some of my favorite alternatives are bite-size bagel pieces and whole grain cereals!

INGREDIENTS:

10–12 cups popped popcorn
½ cup unsalted butter
2 Tbsp. Worcestershire sauce
1 tsp. seasoned salt
1 tsp. garlic powder
1 tsp. onion powder
2 cups pretzel pieces
1 cup peanuts

1. Place popcorn in a large bowl. Remove any unpopped or partially popped kernels.

2. Place butter in a microwave safe bowl and cover with a paper towel. Microwave for 30 seconds at a time until melted. Add Worcestershire sauce, salt, garlic powder, and onion powder. Mix well. Drizzle over popcorn and shake to coat. Add pretzel pieces and peanuts and shake again. Store in an airtight container for up to one week.

Sesame sticks can generally be found where nuts are sold. Look for them near the produce where other salad toppings are located or in the snack aisle next to mixed nuts. If you like spice, try adding 1 teaspoon of hot sauce to spice it up!

INGREDIENTS:

10–12 cups popped popcorn
3 Tbsp. unsalted butter
2 Tbsp. sesame oil
2 Tbsp. honey
2 tsp. soy sauce

½ tsp. garlic powder
¼ tsp. salt
1 Tbsp. sesame seeds
1 cup sesame sticks

1. Place popcorn in a large bowl. Remove any unpopped or partially popped kernels.

2. Place butter in a microwave safe bowl and cover with a paper towel. Microwave for 30 seconds at a time until melted. Add oil, honey, soy sauce, garlic powder, and salt. Mix well. Drizzle over popcorn and shake to coat. Sprinkle with sesame seeds. Add sesame sticks and stir to evenly distribute. Store in an airtight container for up to one week.

SESAME

INGREDIENTS:

10–12 cups popped popcorn
¼ cup buttermilk powder
¼ cup cheese powder
½ tsp. salt
Butter flavored oil spray

1. Place popcorn in a large bowl. Remove any unpopped or partially popped kernels.

2. In a small bowl, mix buttermilk powder, cheese powder, and salt. Spray the top layer of the popcorn with the oil spray and then sprinkle with about 2 tablespoons of the cheese mixture. Stir gently to bring plain popcorn to the surface. Continue spraying with oil and sprinkling with the cheese mixture until fully coated. Store in an airtight container for up to one week.

SOUR CREAM AND CHEDDAR

SOUR CREAM AND ONION

INGREDIENTS:

10–12 cups popped popcorn

¼ cup buttermilk powder

1 Tbsp. onion powder

1½ tsp. salt

1 tsp. crushed dried parsley

½ cup unsalted butter

2 Tbsp. chopped fresh green onions

Buttermilk powder is essential for the sour cream flavor in this recipe. It is generally sold in the baking aisle near the evaporated milk.

1. Place popcorn in a large bowl. Remove any unpopped or partially popped kernels.

2. In a small bowl, mix together buttermilk powder, onion powder, salt, and dried parsley. Set aside.

3. Place butter in a microwave safe bowl and cover with a paper towel. Microwave for 30 seconds at a time until melted. Drizzle over the top of popcorn and shake to coat. Sprinkle spice powder and green onions over popcorn and shake again to coat. Serve immediately.

SRIRACHA AND LIME

Let all your spicy popcorn dreams come true with this Sriracha and Lime Popcorn! If you want it extra spicy, don't increase the sriracha, just add a little cayenne pepper instead!

INGREDIENTS:

10–12 cups popped popcorn
2 Tbsp. unsalted butter
4 tsp. sriracha
2 tsp. lime juice
¼ tsp. chili powder
¼ tsp. salt
2 tsp. lime zest

1. Place popcorn in a large bowl. Remove any unpopped or partially popped kernels.

2. Place butter in a microwave safe bowl and cover with a paper towel. Microwave for 30 seconds at a time until melted. Add sriracha, lime juice, chili powder, salt, and lime zest. Mix well. Drizzle over popcorn and shake to coat. Serve immediately.

SWEET CHILI

Turn up the heat with this Sweet Chili Popcorn. It's the perfect balance of sweet and spicy . . . but it is entirely within your power to change that. Add a little more cayenne pepper if you like things spicy. Add a little more honey if sweet is your thing.

INGREDIENTS:

10–12 cups popped popcorn
½ cup unsalted butter
1 Tbsp. honey
¼ tsp. garlic powder
2 tsp. chili powder

¼ tsp. cayenne pepper
½ tsp salt

1. Place popcorn in a large bowl. Remove any unpopped or partially popped kernels.

2. Place butter in a microwave safe bowl and cover with a paper towel. Microwave for 30 seconds at a time until melted. Add honey and spices. Mix well. Drizzle over popcorn and shake to coat. Serve immediately.

The freshly grated cheese and crispy tortilla strips are the perfect complement to the taco flavored popcorn in this recipe. You can turn this into a make-ahead recipe by keeping the tortilla strips and shredded cheese separate and adding them to the popcorn right before serving.

INGREDIENTS:

10–12 cups popped popcorn   1 cup tortilla strips
½ cup unsalted butter   ½ cup shredded cheese
1.25 oz. packet taco seasoning (about ¼ cup)

1. Place popcorn in a large bowl. Remove any unpopped or partially popped kernels.

2. Place butter in a microwave safe bowl and cover with a paper towel. Microwave for 30 seconds at a time until melted. Drizzle over the top of popcorn and shake to coat. Sprinkle taco seasoning over popcorn and shake again to coat. Add tortilla strips and shredded cheese. Serve immediately.

TACO PIE

THREE CHEESE

INGREDIENTS:

10–12 cups popped popcorn
¼ cup cheese powder
¼ cup parmesan cheese
¼ tsp. salt
Butter flavor oil spray
2 cups cheese crackers

Increase the cheese factor by adding your favorite grated cheeses right before serving! Cheese powder can generally be found in the popcorn aisle or near the spices in the baking aisle of a grocery store.

1. Place popcorn in a large bowl. Remove any unpopped or partially popped kernels.

2. In a small bowl, mix cheese powder, parmesan cheese, and salt. Spray the top layer of the popcorn with the oil spray and then sprinkle with about 2 tablespoons of the cheese mixture. Stir gently to bring plain popcorn to the surface. Continue spraying with oil and sprinkling with the cheese mixture until fully coated. Add cheese crackers and stir to evenly distribute. Store in an airtight container for up to one week.

INGREDIENTS:

10–12 cups popped popcorn

½ cup unsalted butter

½ tsp. salt

1 cup wheat crackers

1 cup total of the following: chia seeds, sunflower seeds, pumpkin seeds, flax seeds, and rolled oats

Nothing says "healthy" quite like whole grains! You can choose your favorite or get a little crazy and mix them all together! Whole grains are often found in the health food sections of regular grocery stores or in bulk bins at health food stores.

1. Place popcorn in a large bowl. Remove any unpopped or partially popped kernels.

2. Place butter in a microwave safe bowl and cover with a paper towel. Microwave for 30 seconds at a time until melted. Add salt and mix well. Drizzle over popcorn and shake to coat. Add wheat crackers and seed mixture and stir to combine. Serve immediately.

WHOLE GRAIN

NOTES